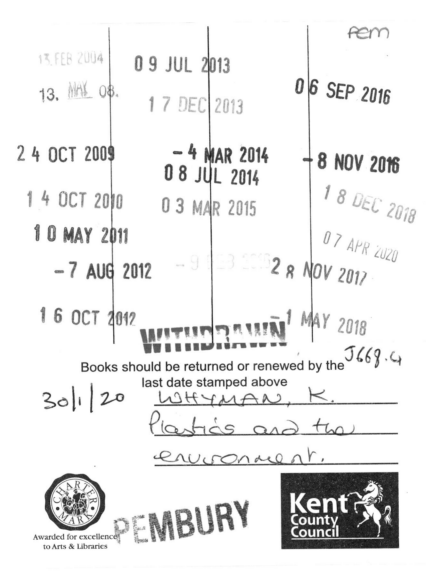

© Archon Press Ltd 2003

Produced by
Archon Books Ltd
28 Percy Street
London W1T 2BZ

New edition first published in
Great Britain in 2003 by
Franklin Watts
96 Leonard Street
London, EC2A 4XD

Original edition published as
Resources Today – Plastics

ISBN 0-7496-4757-4

A CIP catalogue for this book is
available from the British Library

Printed in U.A.E.
All rights reserved

Editor:
Nicola Cameron

Designer:
Phil Kay

Illustrators:
Louise Nevett
Simon Bishop

Picture Researcher:
Brian Hunter Smart

Photocredits Abbreviations: l - left, r - right, b - bottom, t - top, c - centre, m - middle. Cover main, 4t, 4tr, 6t, 6tr, 8t, 8tr, 10t, 12t, 14t, 16t, 18t, 18tr, 20t, 22t, 24t, 26t, 26tr, 28t, 30t, 31t, 32t — Ingram Publishing. Cover c, 19 — Photosource. 1, 23 — Flat Earth. 4-5 — Tony Stone Associates. 9 — Shell Photographic. 12tr — Phil Kay. Cover b, 2-3, 5tr, 10 tr, 11tr, 14tr, 15, 16tr, 20tr, 21tl, 24tr, 24b, 25, 26ml, 27tl, 27b, 28c, 28ml, 28bl, 29t, 29tr, 29mlt, 29 mr, 29mlb, 29bl, 29 br, 30c, 30br — Select Pictures. 17b — NOAA. 18 — Paul Brierley. 21, 22tr — Corbis. 26br — Joe McDonald/CORBIS. 27mr, 28br, 30bm — Digital Stock. 28mr — Scania. 30tr — The Telephone Museum. 30bl — Hulton-Deutsch Collection/CORBIS.

CONTENTS

WHAT IS A PLASTIC?

Plastics are everywhere! As you read this book perhaps you are sitting on a plastic chair, leaning on a plastic-coated table or wearing plastic shoes. There are many different types of plastics. So what makes something a plastic? The first plastics were made more than 100 years ago from cellulose which is naturally found in plants.

Today plastics are made mostly from crude oil, a raw material that is fast running out. In the future, new raw materials must be found to make plastics, and there must be greater recycling of plastic waste.

Plastics are mass produced in factories

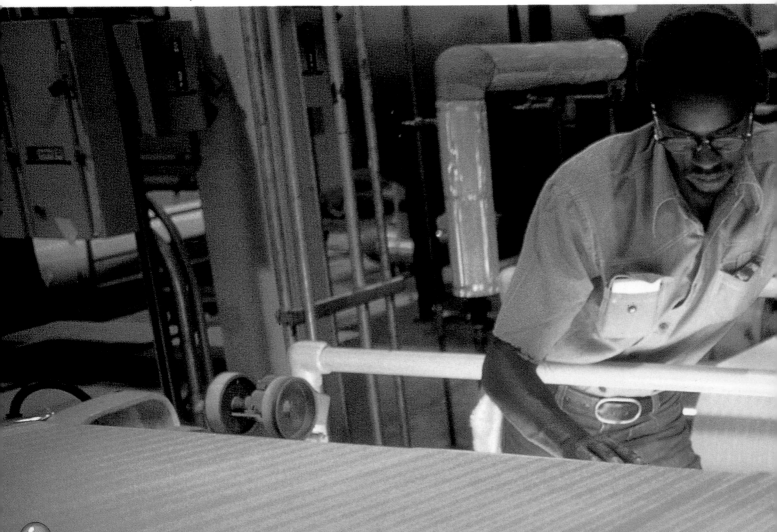

- The word plastic comes from the Greek Plastikos - meaning able to be shaped.

- They can be shaped into almost anything.

- Plastics are light and relatively cheap.

- They can be produced in different colours.

- Heat and electricity do not travel through plastics easily, they are good 'insulators' .

- Unlike metals and wood, they do not rust or rot.

But plastics do have some disadvantages too.

- They are made from resources which will eventually run out, and they are difficult to recycle.

- Because they do not naturally rot (biodegrade) like wood, they are an eyesore and a hazard in the environment.

- They are not as strong as many metals and they melt at high temperatures, sometimes giving off poisonous fumes.

WHERE DO PLASTICS COME FROM?

Most plastics come from chemicals in crude oil. However as the world's reserves of crude oil begin to run out, coal and gas are now being used more frequently. At a refinery, crude oil is separated into different fractions or chemicals. Most of these fractions are used for fuels.

In a further process at the refinery some of the remaining fractions are cracked or separated into various parts, including the gas ethylene, one of the main chemicals from which plastics can be made.

A refinery where thousands of tonnes of oil are processed

WHAT HAPPENS AT AN OIL REFINERY?

• Crude oil is piped in and heated. As the different chemicals (or 'fractions') in the oil get hotter they start to boil and turn into gases (or 'evaporate').

• Each fraction boils at a different temperature. The ones with the lowest boiling points stay as gases for longest. They rise to the top of the column as they cool. The liquids with higher boiling points do not stay as gases for long, so they do not rise far.

• As each gas cools it turns back into a liquid (or 'condenses'). The condensing liquids are collected at different levels in the column.

• Oil is full of useful chemicals. Did you know we get fuels, soaps, tar and some of the ingredients for drugs from the chemicals in oil?

• Certain fractions are mixed to give plastic making chemicals.

Crude oil

Heat applied

Petroleum gases

COOLER TOP

Petrols (gasolines)

Jet fuels (kerosene) and paraffin

Diesel oils

Light lubricating and fuel oils

Heavy, thick fuel and lubricating oils

Waxes and bitumens

HOW ARE PLASTICS MADE?

In a polymerisation reactor, pressure and heat cause ethylene molecules, mixed with other chemicals, to link together. In ethylene the molecules form a colourless inflammable gas. When the same molecules are linked together in big chains called polymers, the plastic polyethylene or polythene is made – one of the world's most widely used plastics. Other chemical combinations can produce polymers of different lengths and structures.

Once the polymers have been formed, the hot liquid plastic is taken from the reactor, cooled, and cut into chips or pellets.

Ethylene molecules

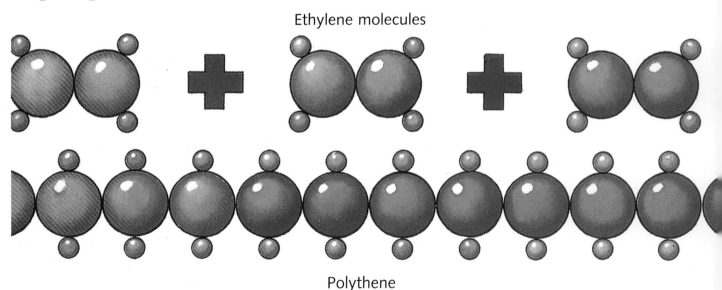

Polythene

- Each molecule of ethylene is made up of two atoms of carbon and four of hydrogen. The top part of the diagram shows three of these molecules.

- If another chemical, known as a 'catalyst', is added these molecules form a long chain. This is called 'polymerisation'.

- Polythene gets its name from 'poly' meaning 'many'.

Most plastics are made from oil. Polystyrene is often used for packaging (inset).

TYPES OF PLASTIC

Although there are many different types of plastic, they can all be divided into two main groups. These are called 'thermoplastics' and 'thermosetting plastics'. Thermoplastics include polypropylene, polystyrene, polyester, acrylics and nylons. These types of plastic melt when heated and become solid again as they cool. Thermosetting plastics do not behave in this way. Bakelite and melamine are both thermosetting plastics.

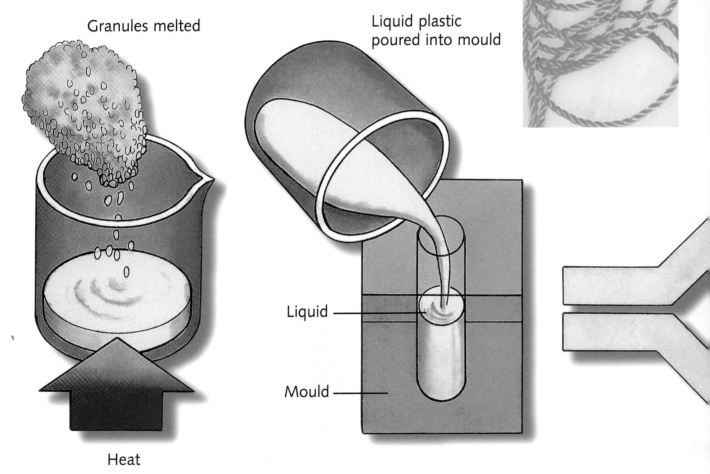

Granules melted

Liquid plastic poured into mould

Liquid

Mould

Heat

• When plastics are made they are either in the form of a thick liquid or solid granules. This material is called 'raw plastic'.

• The granules are tipped into a container and heated until they melt. They may contain a colouring dye.

• The liquid plastic is then poured into a mould. The shape inside the mould is exactly the same shape as the finished article.

• Until this point the thermoplastics and the thermosetting plastics are treated in the same way.

Thermoplastics are often used for clothing and packaging material, both of which can be recycled. Thermosetting plastics are resistant to high temperatures. For this reason they are often used to make saucepan handles and ashtrays.

The strong polymer links of the thermosetting plastic mean that it holds its shape even when heated. Plastics of this kind cannot be melted down and used again easily.

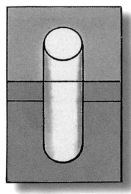

These compact discs have been made from thermosetting plastic.

THERMOSETTING PLASTICS

• When the thermosetting plastic is heated, links form between the polymers in the plastic. They become joined together into a permanent structure.

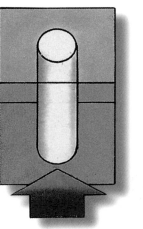

Heat

Cooled

Solid cannot be reshaped

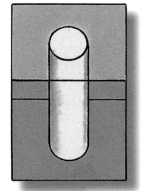

Cooled

Solid – can be reshaped

THERMOPLASTICS

• The thermoplastic, however, has different types of links and can be melted down and used again.

MOULDING PLASTICS

Many different objects are made from plastic – thin sheets for wrapping food, long strips for curtain rails, hollow bottles and complicated toys. With such a huge range of items made of plastic it is not surprising that there are many different ways of moulding plastic.

Some of the most common ways of moulding or 'setting' thermoplastics are shown below. The method used depends on the type of article being made.

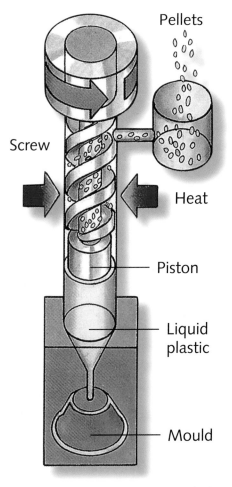

Pellets

Screw

Heat

Piston

Liquid plastic

Mould

• Granules of plastic are fed into a heated tube. A piston forces the liquid plastic down and out into a mould where it cools and hardens.

• If a hollow, thin shape is being made, 'dip moulding' may be the best method. Here a solid mould is dipped into a liquid plastic paste.

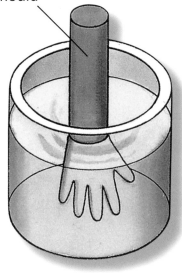

Glove mould

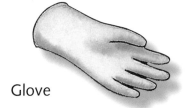

Glove

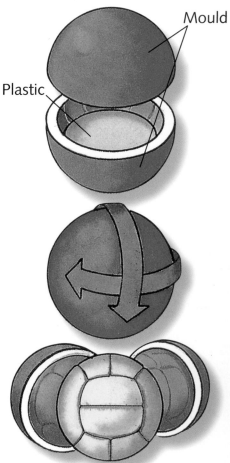

Mould

Plastic

• Beach balls are often made by 'rotational casting'. Plastic powder is fed into a rotating mould. When the mould is heated, a strong plastic coating forms on the inside.

• In 'extrusion', molten thermoplastic is forced through a hole. The shape of the hole or 'die' determines the articles' shape.

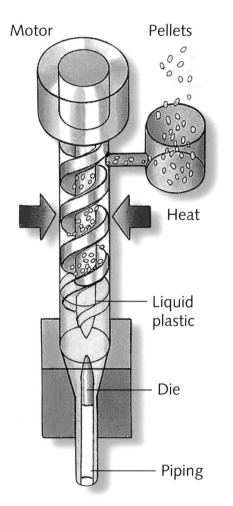

Motor

Pellets

Heat

Liquid plastic

Die

Piping

Heat

Sheet

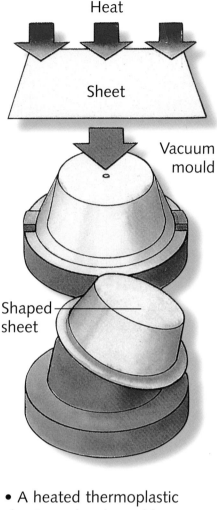

Vacuum mould

Shaped sheet

• A heated thermoplastic sheet can be shaped by 'vacuum moulding'. As air is drawn out, the sheet is sucked into the mould.

• In 'blow moulding', a thin tube of thermoplastic is extruded and sealed at one end. Air is blasted into the tube, forcing the plastic into the mould.

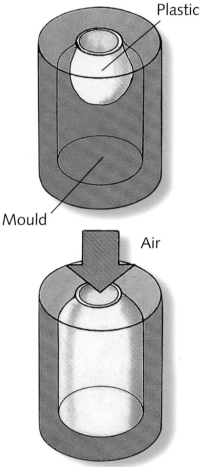

Plastic

Mould

Air

Moulded thermoplastics

Many thermosetting plastics must be heated in order to mould them. This is called 'heat compression moulding'. The mould is usually made of steel and is held in a press in two pieces. Plastic is placed in the lower part of the mould and the two pieces are then pressed (or 'compressed') together. As the mould is heated the plastic softens to fill every part of the mould. It is then left to harden in the press.

MAKING HARD SHEETS

Plastics are not always moulded into shapes – we often need sheets of plastic. Perspex is a thermosetting plastic, ideal for making windows and roof lights. Perspex is as clear as glass and does not break easily. It is made by pouring liquid plastic between two sheets of sealed glass. When the glass sheets are clamped together and passed through a hot oven, the plastic sheet hardens to form perspex.

Table tops and other surfaces are sometimes protected with sheets called 'laminates'. Melamine is a laminate. This thermosetting plastic forms a very strong, tough surface. Melamine is resistant to heat and does not stain easily.

Glass fibre reinforcement

Plastic resin

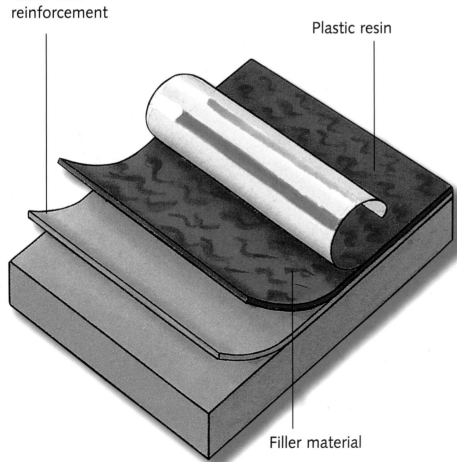

Filler material

Laminates

• Laminates are made up of different layers of thin sheets of materials.

• Some plastic laminates contain a plastic resin, a glass fibre reinforcement and filler material such as paper.

• Laminates are moulded under heat and pressure to form a hard-wearing, heat resistant material.

• Melamine and polyester are some of the plastics used to make laminates.

• Laminates are often used to make tabletops and household flooring.

Hard sheets of plastic can be moulded into many different shapes

MAKING FLEXIBLE SHEETS

Laminates and perspex are both hard. Different plastics are needed to make flexible sheets. Carrier bags, light raincoats, shower curtains and food packaging are just some of the products made from plastic sheets.

Food and other articles are often 'shrink wrapped'. The article is wrapped and sealed in a thin plastic film that has been heated, stretched and then cooled. Although the film stays stretched when it cools, if the wrapped article is passed through a hot tunnel, the plastic melts and shrinks back to its original size, wrapping the item very tightly.

• Polythene sheets are usually made by a sort of extrusion called the 'tubular film process'.
• Raw plastic pellets are heated and the molten plastic is forced through a tube.
• A jet of cold air is blown through the tube making it blow up like a balloon.
• The plastic is then stretched into thin sheets.

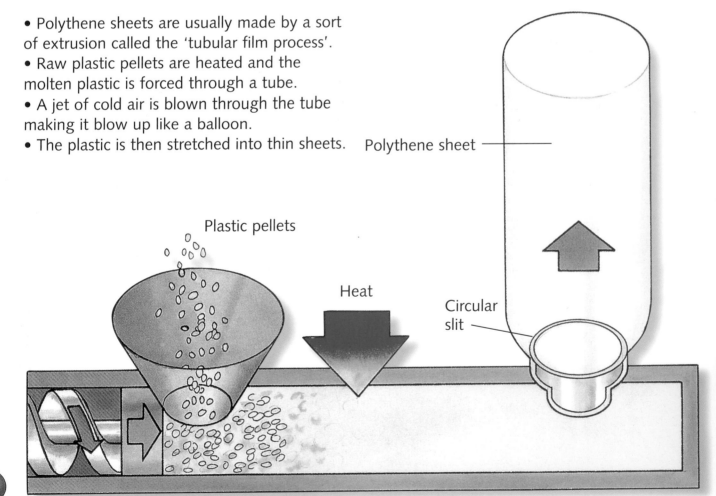

Plastic pellets

Heat

Polythene sheet

Circular slit

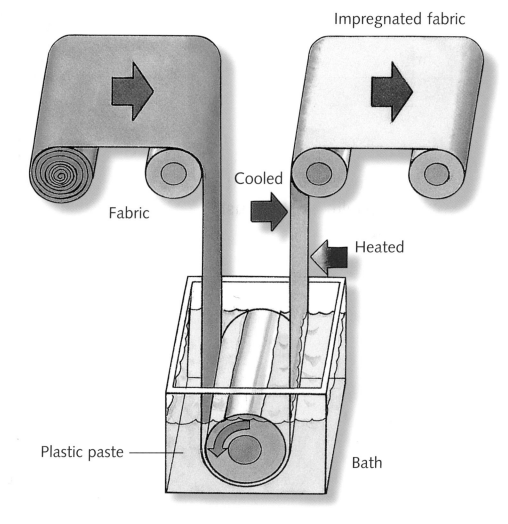

Impregnated fabric

Fabric

Cooled

Heated

Plastic paste

Bath

HOW TO MAKE WATERPROOF MATERIALS

• Fabrics can be made waterproof by soaking or 'impregnating' them with plastic. The fabric is wound round a roller which is in a bath of plastic paste. The plastic soaks into the fabric.

• The fabric is wound out of the bath, heated and then cooled. The plastic is now set and the fabric is wound onto rollers ready to be made into waterproof products such as raincoats or tents.

• The fabrics may be coated with plastic on one side. This is called 'calendering'.

Waterproof clothing is made from flexible plastic or material that has been coated with plastic

PAINTS AND ADHESIVES

Did you know that paints and adhesives contain plastics? Paints are often made of three different chemicals. A 'pigment' provides the colour; a plastic holds the pigment in place and gives a shiny finish; and a 'solvent', usually white spirit, makes the paint runny and easy to use. When the paint dries, the solvent evaporates and only the pigment and plastic are left.

Strong glues like 'superglue' are made of thermosetting plastics called epoxy resins. They can stick metal, glass, china, wood – in fact almost anything!

Glues made from thermosetting plastics can set without heating

Some paints contain plastic to bind the pigment

FOAMS

Bubbles and air can be put into plastics to turn them into foams and lightweight plastics. Sometimes the bubbles are big enough to see. In other cases they are microscopic. Plastic foams have a number of uses. They are excellent materials for insulating and for making packaging like cartons for foods, toys and delicate items which need protecting from knocks.

Rigid foam is mainly used as a heat insulator. It is injected into the spaces between the outer walls of houses to keep them warmer. Some plastic foams can be toxic due to the chemicals involved in making them. Now, many foams are made which are less toxic.

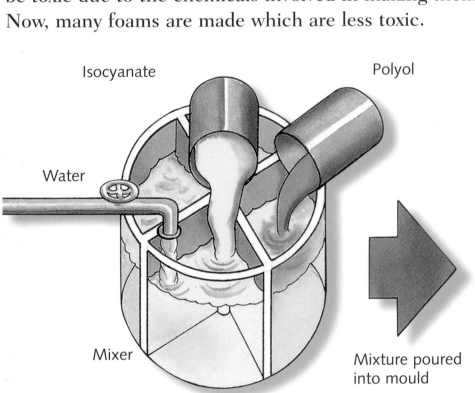

Isocyanate

Polyol

Water

Mixer

Mixture poured into mould

Carbon gas forms 'bubbles'

Making Polyurethane

• Isocyanate and Polyol, two chemicals, are mixed together with an acid and a foaming agent to form polyurethane.

• The mixture froths and sets almost immediately into a lightweight rigid foam.

• Styrofoam (foamed polystyrene) is another bubble filled foam, where the blowing chemical is heated to form bubbles.

Making sheets of foam in a factory. Foam can be used as a cushion in the inside of a crash helmet.

SYNTHETIC FIBRES

Plastics are used to make synthetic fabrics for clothes, curtains, sheets and carpets. Nylon, polyester and acrylic are all plastic fabrics. They are made from thermoplastics. You may wonder why it is necessary to make synthetic fabrics when there are natural ones, like cotton and wool. The answer is that natural fabrics from raw materials are expensive and in short supply.

Clothes made from synthetic fabrics have other advantages such as they do not crease much. However, they are not so comfortable to wear, or as warm, as natural fabrics. Synthetic fabrics are often mixed with natural ones to combine the advantages of both.

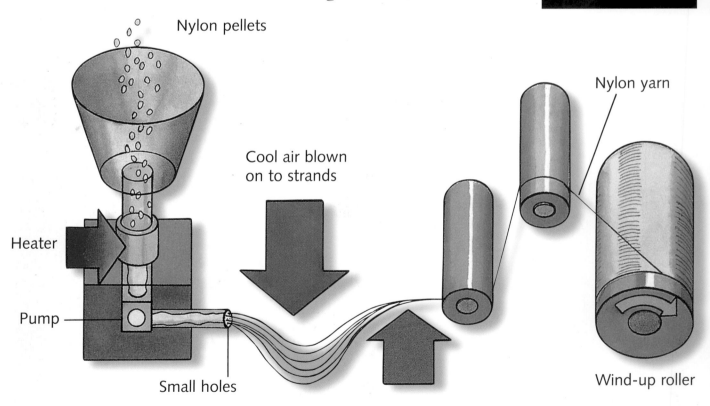

Nylon pellets

Cool air blown on to strands

Nylon yarn

Heater

Pump

Small holes

Wind-up roller

• The long threads, or 'fibres', used to make synthetic fabrics are made by the extrusion process. The diagram shows nylon fibres being made by a process called 'melt spinning'.

• The plastic pellets are melted and forced through very fine holes in a machine called a 'spinneret'. The fibres harden as they cool and are wound onto a roller, ready to be woven.

Synthetic fibres are also used to make carpets

RECYCLING

We throw away millions of tonnes of plastics every year. Plastics make up about one-tenth of the weight of waste thrown away. Most of this is buried as landfill rubbish under layers of earth. Many plastics do not rot or break down naturally. This means that plastic rubbish will remain on our planet for a very long time.

Recycling is the process of re-using waste materials to make new products. However, recycling plastics is complicated. Different types of plastic need to be processed in different ways. Some plastics can be melted and used to make more plastic products such as bags and bottles. Others can be made into fibres for clothing. Some can be burned as fuel in the recycling process.

 Plastic does not degrade naturally in the environment

A small section of the huge amount of plastics in a landfill site

THE ENVIRONMENT

Plastics are derived from natural resources – oil, coal and natural gas. We are using oil so fast that the Earth's supplies may run out within 100 years. If they do, so will plastics. Scientists are investigating new ideas for making plastics by processing plants such as the sweet potato, bamboo and flax. Using organic raw materials to make plastics would be kinder to the environment. Items such as a car would be easier to dispose of. If a car was made of organic raw materials most of the parts would naturally rot. Instead of scrapping it, you may just end up eating it!

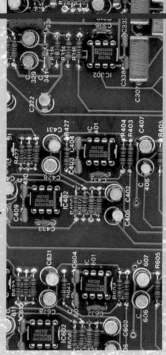

▼ Wildlife

Plastics can be extremely hazardous to wildlife. Each year, many birds become entangled in plastic drinks can holders. Once the plastic is wrapped around a bird's neck or feet, it is difficult to escape. This causes panic and, ultimately, death.

▲ Pollution

The Trabant emerged in the 1950s as one of the first cars to be made almost entirely out of plastic. While its benefits included value for money and a vehicle that would not easily rust, it also had its downfalls. The plastic used on this car would not breakdown naturally in the environment and so disposal was difficult. Unfortunately, the Trabant added to the mass waste in landfill sites.

Re-using

Large water containers like these can be re-used many times. This is far more considerate to the environment than disposing of numerous smaller bottles each time you have a drink.

It's also a good idea to donate old computers, compact discs, video tapes, toys and household goods to charity shops for re-use.

▶ Alternative sources

Plastics are made from natural resources that are not renewable. These resources are rapidly running out. Alternative sources such as soya beans and sugars can be processed into plastic products, saving our valuable non-renewable sources.

◀ What you can do

Look for alternative materials or avoid excess packaging when shopping. When you recycle your plastics, try to separate the different colours as this saves much time and energy in the melt. Many plastics can be recycled, even your old toys. Just because they don't work, it doesn't mean that they can't be re-used!

PLASTICS AND THEIR USES

Plastics have so many uses and many also have different names. These names include the brand names, trade names, manufacturers' names and the inventor's name. The unique characteristics of plastics mean that an enormous variety of products can be made, such as hard and flexible sheets, foams and fabrics as well as moulded objects. Plastics are an important part of everyday life.

Thermoplastics	Characteristics
Acrylonitrile-butadiene-styrene (ABS)	Very tough and resists impact. It is used for pipes, tubing, car parts, protective equipment, tools, casing, small appliances and fridge door linings.
Acrylic (PMMA)	Hard, strong and transparent. It is used in clothing, as it is cheaper to produce than natural textiles, and in reflectors, paints, signs and safety 'glass'. 
Celluloid 	The first thermoplastic: a substance moulded under heat and pressure into a shape. Celluloid went on to be used in the first flexible photographic film and in making movies.
Polycarbonate	A clear, strong material which is used for windows, safety 'glass', household and office equipment and traffic signs. 
Polyethylene (polythene) 	Adaptable, flexible and durable. Low-density polyethylene is used for plastic bags, films and bottles. High-density is used for crates, pressure equipment and plastic piping.

Thermoplastics		Characteristics

Polytetrafluoro-ethylene (PTFE, Teflon)

Resistant to heat, chemicals and electricity. Teflon is used for heat-resistant and non-stick coatings and surfaces as well as in insulation.

Polypropylene

Tough and flexible. Polypropylene is used in making ropes for binding, pipes, tubes, household equipment and medical products such as artificial joints.

Polystyrene

Light and brittle, but when made into a foamed version, polystyrene is suitable to be used for packaging and in floating items such as lifejackets.

Polyvinyl chloride (PVC) or 'vinyl'

Strong, adaptable and resistant to sunlight and weather. Polyvinyl is used in clothes, window frames, flooring and as artificial leather.

Thermosetting plastics

Epoxy-resin plastics

Strong, durable and hard. Epoxy-resins are used for electrical equipment, flooring, sports gear and as glues.

Phenol-formaldehyde (Bakelite, melamine)

Tough, heat-resistant, shatter-proof. Bakelite will not crease, crack or discolour from exposure to sunlight. It is used for domestic purposes such as electrical insulators.

Polyurethane

Polyurethane makes good foam and is good for insulation, sports equipment, padding and furniture. It is also ideal for packaging to protect items from being knocked or bumped during transportation.

PLASTICS AND THEIR HISTORY

The first plastic-type material was unveiled by Alexander Parkes at the Great International Exhibition in London in 1862. Parkes claimed that his new material could do anything that rubber was capable of, but at a much lower price. This material could be moulded into thousands of different shapes.

▲ Bakelite telephone
In 1907, a New York chemist, Leo Bakeland, created a liquid resin which he named Bakelite. This resin could be moulded into any shape and it would not burn, boil or melt when it was set. Bakelite was the first thermosetting plastic which would always keep its shape and form.

Cellophane ▶
In 1913, Dr Jacques Edwin Brandenberger invented a wipeable surface by adding a clear, flexible film to cloth. Brandenberger invented cellophane. Now it is widely used for packaging and is a fully flexible, waterproof wrap.

▲ Nylon stockings
In 1939, nylon stockings were unveiled and were extremely popular with many women during the war years (1939-1945). Nylon replaced animal hair in toothbrushes, and silk in stockings.

▼ Kevlar®
In a laboratory in 1965, two research scientists created a new fibre. They named it Kevlar®. It was strong, light and flexible. Today it is used for sports equipment, bullet-proof vests and for ropes used on the expedition to Mars.

▲ Velcro®
In 1957, George de Maestral was so impressed with the way that cocklebars – a type of vegetation – used thousands of tiny hooks to cling to anything, he invented a product, using nylon, that would replicate this natural phenomenon. He called it Velcro®.

GLOSSARY

Biodegrade
To rot, or break down naturally in the enviroment by the action of moulds and other living organisms.

Catalyst
A chemical which helps a chemical reaction take place more easily.

Celluloid
A flammable thermoplastic usually mixed with camphor. Used in plastic sheets such as cinema and photographic film.

Cellulose
A natural substance found in plant materials such as cotton and wood. Used to make a plastic called celluloid.

Cracking
The process of breaking and re-shaping molecules by heating with catalyst in an oil refinery.

Extrusion
When a substance is pulled or drawn out into a long, thin shape, such as a tube.

Foam
A substance that contains air and bubbles. Foamed plastic is a solid-based foam. Soap makes a liquid-based foam.

Insulation
Resisting or preventing the flow of heat (thermal insulation) or electricity (electrical insulation).

Landfill site
A place where waste material is disposed of by burying it under layers of earth.

Mould
A hollow structure into which molten or soft material is poured and then allowed to harden. Moulds can make different shaped objects.

Petroleum
Crude oil – the thick, dark coloured, flammable liquid found in rocks below the Earth's surface.

Pigment
A substance which is added to give things their colour.

Polymer
A large group of molecules, made from many smaller molecules (monomers) joined together.

Raw plastic
Material which has not yet completed the process of becoming a plastic object.

Recycling
The process of re-using waste materials to make new products.

Resins
Substances which come from the sap of some trees and other plants. Synthetic resin is a type of plastic.

Solvent
A substance, usually a liquid, which is able to dissolve other substances.

Synthetic
A material which has been artificially made by chemical reaction, as opposed to natural materials such as cotton and wood.

Thermoplastic
A synthetic plastic or resin which becomes soft when heated and rehardens when cooled.

Thermosetting plastic
A synthetic plastic which hardens permanently after being heated. Once set, it cannot be remoulded.

Toxic
Poisonous. A toxin, or poison, is harmful or deadly.

INDEX